A PIECE OF GOOD NEWS

FARRAR STRAUS GIROUX

NEW YORK

KATIE PETERSON

A PIECE OF GOOD NEWS

Farrar, Straus and Giroux
175 Varick Street, New York 10014

Printed in the United States of America
First edition, 2019

Library of Congress Cataloging-in-Publication Data
Names: Peterson, Katie, 1974– author.
Title: A piece of good news : poems / Katie Peterson.
Description: First edition. | New York : Farrar, Straus and Giroux, 2019.
Identifiers: LCCN 2018031293 | ISBN 9780374232795 (hardcover)
Classification: LCC PS3616.E8429 A6 2019 | DDC 811/.6—dc23
LC record available at https://lccn.loc.gov/2018031293

Designed by Quemadura

Our books may be purchased in bulk for promotional, educational,
or business use. Please contact your local bookseller or the Macmillan
Corporate and Premium Sales Department at 1-800-221-7945, extension
5442, or by e-mail at MacmillanSpecialMarkets@macmillan.com.

www.fsgbooks.com
www.twitter.com/fsgbooks
www.facebook.com/fsgbooks

1 3 5 7 9 10 8 6 4 2

FOR MY HUSBAND

&

IN MEMORY OF MY MOTHER

—PLATO, *Phaedo*, trans. G.M.A. Grube

Very well, Socrates, what are your instructions to me and the others about your children or anything else? What can we do that would please you most?

Nothing new, Crito, said Socrates, but what I am always saying, that you will please me and mine and yourselves by taking good care of your own selves in whatever you do, even if you do not agree with me now, but if you neglect your own selves, and are unwilling to live following the tracks, as it were, of what we have said now and on previous occasions, you will achieve nothing even if you strongly agree with me at this moment.

CONTENTS

A PIECE OF GOOD NEWS

THE BORDER

I had a lust for what was distant.
We were in love. We crossed the border
in broad daylight and the color
of the currency deepened
but didn't change. The night before
we made love in my sister's bed.

The coastline shivered and the wind
picked up. You lit a cigarette
inside the car. The potholes
made a song of ruin
so consistent no one noticed.
Vacation homes more proximate

than gas stations. The language
on the radio didn't change.
When I was hungry you took me to the movies.

When I was tired we went looking
for a shopping mall to purchase
a pair of shoes like the locals

wear—not local. Later we chose a bar
because someone shouted at us.
You felt guilty I paid a man
to shine my tall black boots
but kept staring at the stripper
who must have rubbed her breasts

with lotion before she came to work.
The whole way home, I was never sicker.
I drank the water. I thought it was okay.
We talked about people we fucked
when we should have been
sleeping with each other.

PLEASURE

I remembered what it was like,
knowing what you want to eat and then making it,
forgetting about the ending in the middle,
looking at the ocean for
a long time without restlessness,
or with restlessness not inhabiting the joints,
sitting Indian-style on a porch
overlooking the water, smooth like good cake frosting.
And then I experienced it, falling so deeply
into the story line, I laughed as soon as the character
    entered
the picture, humming the theme music even when I'd
    told myself
I wanted to be quiet and not talk forever.
And I thought, *Now is the right time to cut up your shirt.*

I wanted to be seen. But who would see me? I couldn't
think of the name for anything but a flower. The
   government
makes coins that size and shape so your hand can feel
safe holding them. The pictures stamped remind
us where we are, or how the landscape
we live in connects itself, through a common value,
to a different place. On this one, a spinnaker
sails past a bridge. On that, a diamond shines like a child's
stilled top over a bird, as if the diamond made the rest of the
   natural
world — bird, forest, state flower, sheaf of healthy corn,
   shining
water — out of proportion in relation to itself. I love this.
   My own state
has a bear, so small and out of proportion to me that my life-
line crosses behind it. At last I do not fear
that but feel proud the animal can sit in my palm so silently

until I spend it. And if I lose it, it becomes
even more quiet. Most still just have an eagle,
so, it is as if thirty eagles were passed over
from one hand to another when the one
charged with arranging things for his Savior's dinner
arranged his Savior's death. Heavier the yoke
of heat in solitude. A walk uphill does not
feel manageable. Who will see me?

OPERA

The next morning, I tried to remember her face, but her dress
sailed into the center of my eye, a ship luscious with sail
crossing no horizon but stopping where I knew
my nose was, that ridiculous mountain
only lovers find right ways to compliment. But then I tried
harder to call it back, and my eyes rose to meet her
décolletage and her shoulders and the manner
in which her clavicle hinged at her neck to sing
with such dexterity she could stomach a world
of old and rich and earnest admirers.
And so, what I remembered came from a pose
I can recall, though his hands were around me in such a way
I could only watch sideways and still be loved,
and what I remembered could not be said
to appear at once at the top of a tall tree
like the endangered condor from a hiding place in some
    remote part

of California, or, likewise, over the ocean like a salt-crusted
   hawk.
She made the most sexual face I had ever seen
when she described why she sold her possessions.

They had decided against it,
but then they entered the field of sunflowers
together after some pictures had been taken
with a storm in the background,
the shape of a fist, and wrinkled like a raisin,
the color of the strong liquor made from raisins
they had yet to taste or buy. They entered
the field of sunflowers by pushing
through an avenue of stalks.
Her hair blows south-southwest,
the difficult girl who's just been centered
by the lens of the easy boy,
and I am in the corner of the picture.
Each kilometer cost more than we knew.
He asked her to translate the American
films they watched in French
back into English. He wanted to hear
the meaning of what she remembered, doubled.

I wanted her to admit she posed
for the picture. I could see him beginning
to study happiness, how its large blue eyes
set limits on pleasure, but my one regret
from that summer was not cutting the stalk
of at least one sunflower so I could
see water ache from its insides.
We were heading towards a vineyard
of uncertain reputation. A translation
told us to find Street of the Mill.
Street of the Well was all we could discover.
Find a road and take it, keep
some conviction about your destination
though the evidence says the whole
thing's going south. In the picture,
the girl could be my double, but her chin
tilts west towards the storm and I
am tacking north, towards a city
where a garden named for a smaller country
fills with locals drinking golden aperitifs.

How do I begin to describe what it was? It was a terrible time to be on a horse. It wasn't a family. I had no brothers. No one told me about the wind. The animals kept us honest. I believed most in friendship, its promises and disappointments. I had hopes for it, expectations. I fell in love too late with what I loved.

THE FOUNTAIN

Dark green water, reflection of the grove
of elms and pines, at the end of summer,
with a woman standing in it, a statue of a woman,
and a spray of water rising and falling,
the fiction of a natural spring.

Her arms raised in a pose of remembering
some invocation to a god of beauty, and her legs
twisted, with the right before the left
so her thighs, under her dress, give her hips a pose and give
her torso the elegance of intended height.

She laughs the laurel garland off
her hair, almost, and since her hair is stone,
the askew of the wreath
indicates an unseen wind, the kind that might
visit a vineyard in a country

where currency can never be broken
into coin, where the midday
meal has at least three courses and finishes
with the ripest plums, not an assortment
but a selection of one kind of good fruit.

But time was made beside the glassy pool,
its sunken keyhole troubled by the motion of its waters,
waters that served as a mirror
much clearer than the fountain,
where the woman steadied her laurel

with her left hand, and with her right
chose more flowers, small wild white roses, for a garland
around her neck. That's where you'd rather be on a hot day.
Each morning she comes here, but some she doesn't
rise early from her bower in those trees, the pines

with their outrageous verticals,
their insistence on arranging partial views,
through columns that exclude as much as frame,
cutting off the hillside, amputating
some people's progress

towards her part of the landscape. Some days she lies
late with her maker there,
though she is stone. He cradles her. There should be a word
for when events are natural
but their order makes no sense. He falls asleep

with his left hand on her breast, thinking
of his chisel and the block of marble
he left uncut to attend to this job
I suspect he only did for pay. I am happy
when I walk down my sloping lawn

to my fountain, in the morning
in the middle of the summer, I won't admit
we are close to the end.
I am happy, and as you can see, my pride
has nothing to do

with anything I ever could have made.

THE MASSACHUSETTS
BOOK OF THE DEAD

In Massachusetts, the sun of winter
is disappearing behind a fragile field
of cloud like Emily Dickinson
rising from the bedclothes to fasten
her corset and stay inside all day.

Sun, make yourself a silence on this house.
If my eyes are closed I am not sleeping. If they
are open let them rest
in between
the delicate snowflakes.

My mother died at nine o'clock at night.
I will be awake
past my bedtime forever.

When a picture of her gets fixed on
by my mind, even the fence that separates
this blue house from that blue house
divides itself into original planks,
reminds me that the tree began as trunk.

We should not go out when it's like this.
As if not going out makes this a home.

Still, fresh produce fills the aisles of March.
Even as winter tires itself out.

What made the scholar remember the name
of the black paramour of the white news anchor
was what caused her to forget the length of time
her lover took to tie her up in leather,
anticipating the denouement of pleasure.

It is better the Atlantic and Pacific
do not cohabitate. Their arguments
over the origin of grains of sand
made the children think it was their fault.
Thus the flatness of tedious Ohio.

Abstain from intercourse anticipating storms,
from sex, abstain, she told herself,
looping with a homemade recording
the movement of the Schubert sonata
she loved most, that allegretto
whose architecture tells you how he died.

He said that when he fucked her he could feel
the orchards of California in their lines
of absences and branches, and branches.

The glass door to her office bore a pattern
of vines and apples and the shadow
of a woman sometimes appeared there
as if in a children's puzzle book

opened in a doctor's waiting room,
waiting for her eye doctor to turn
her eye back towards her nose
with a prescription for double bifocals.

The anguish of the river breaking apart.
Someone told me about it on the phone.

The graveyard lay a short walk through the wood
behind the Homestead. Hale and ruddy,
the Irishmen who stewarded her casket
to the gate did not find themselves out of breath.
One wondered, *Was she even inside?*
Apples on high branches. Midsummer.

The sense of the past and the pastoral
are not one sense. But past the outskirts
of the city, the fences fall away:
foundations of a house,
occupied by moss.

The trunk of the wet pine in the yard
crushed the crossbeam of the kitchen,
made hash of the skylight where the rain
drummed itself out for decades.
We spoke of the repair in whispers.

Said of the recluse: she loved music
drifting up the staircase that she saw
as the only portal to a world
whose code of conduct she disdained
as minor chords disdain a major scale.

Her shopping list, years after she was gone.
The pleasure of organizing need.

Halfway through the entirety of *The Great Gatsby*
read onstage by actors in the mock office
of a dentist in downtown Dubuque,
the scholar fell asleep
dreaming of her last Gauloises, before she quit.

She could see the border from her house.
But where exactly did the horizon end?

Be decent and put on your moccasins.

I walked the Eastern Coast with my Western father
combing the cumulus
for signs of sunlight or signs of rain.

The young man buys a vinyl for his girl
who does not purchase rubbers for them both,
having been prescribed some pills for that.
He recycles her bottle of vitaminwater
watching a crested yellow flicker.

When I sleep fetal I sleep the best.
When I say *likeness*
I am referring to *myself*
considered as a form of happiness.

The difference between disintegration
and what was never true.

I was angry as the tree outside your window
split in half by a rusty sash thrown open in shitty weather.

By this I mean I was like everyone else.

At the end of all my education
about the literature of Massachusetts,
I knew Melville almost as well as Melville
knew women.

We were eating dumplings and discussing
whether history could happen without progress.
In the same way a river might appear
to hurtle between the walls of a Western canyon
neither away from nor towards any source.

The recluse had a reputation for making
delectable gingerbread of a texture
perfect for crumbling on a cold afternoon
into a cup of tea with milk and sugar.
A good way to make people come to her.

You could take your revenge on life
by living more years of it, sheer persistence.
You could fish the map instead of the river.
You could drink a boiling cup of tea
and burn your throat into a sunset.

PROVISIONING

We were provisioning. I thought we needed more.
The road black on either side, in both directions,
until we arrived at a fragile junction:
stop sign and supermarket: each crossroads
brings sustenance and holds an argument.
We stopped at the grocery store for liquor.
Almost letting ourselves be tired,
we continued. The argument concerned

the public and the private.
Where we should live. Snow
descended on the windows of the vehicle,
refraining not accumulating rhythm.
The wipers brushed all of it away
towards one side and two ranges of mountains.
The older hiding the base of the taller.
The taller the kind that tempts a climber.

I think my father made his peace
with death on one of those peaks once.
I think he has forgotten. We could finish
the drive up the backside
of the Sierra in a day. I loved
the names of those lonely places that we passed
so much I felt ashamed to let my mouth
linger over syllables: *Adelanto*.

Nothing could convince me
anything was fragile. I saw my breath
against the windows, towards the last pass,
beginning with the chute that goes straight up
towards the first trees of the bristlecone forest.
Then the road turns topsy-turvy
before it levels out, a mile-long tabletop
summit. Anybody wants to speed there.

If you do, you miss the single boot
hung from a pine tree for no reason.
After that the road becomes a gully.
You drove faster than I even noticed.
I noticed. You kept going.

We argued about what we should love.
Beauty must be witnessed to exist.
I took the opposite position.

I took the side of the icicle
melting at midnight on a day
when work had taken it out of everyone
sweet enough to notice.
We stopped looking at each other.
I know your cheekbone and your forehead
by the argument they make.
Right now it is two winters later.

January: a fragile domesticity.
I have no idea what to eat.
Two winters. We continued
into the valley. We mended
the argument. The cows bedded down
in the frozen sage
with their identical animal children.
You opened a cold beer. The cat had missed me.

The owl found a visible shelter
in spite of two handfuls of snow

collecting in the juncture two cottonwood branches
made into a perch by their separation
from a trunk whose isolate location
made the owl easy to see.
Two in the morning, you didn't want to touch me.
The next day, you wanted to do everything.

God wasn't my father, so I kept lookout
for him while he went
with women who weren't his wife. I wasn't

his desire, so when I got caught,
nothing kept me
from punishment, and my tongue

found a new home at the bottom
of a river already rich with victims
and fish. We were never

as together as the night I lost my voice
for hiding his pleasure,
his going so far into the body of a mortal

and coming out, his masquerade
of manliness as masculinity wasn't enough.
His fingers on her

watery gown made current
of that river,
one rivulet of strap, and then another,

and then the girl was done, the bed
of that river unmade,
if you want to keep

that metaphor
and I do.
I like a metaphor to stay

conventional, to have been used. I ran
to my mother
since I'd woken without speaking.

When she looked into my mouth,
she gasped. I saw
her open

mouth ringed in teeth lose all
its rose and close, her hopes
for me dashed. I was past

even a "shouldn't have done,"
past being
sent to sleep without dinner. I call

this growing up. You have to pay
but never to the right person. She had stayed
up all night, waiting

for me. I loved my mother,
but lost my language
for a trashy god, and that's the truth.

So I learned to listen
again. It meant to translate
wildly. To imitate is never

enough for the listener
who desires
participation. I gained

the power
to repeat, repetition
became a way of life,

I will always be in school

I became required to reply
in exactly the words I heard.
Everything in me, of its own

volition, would strain
towards the intonation the words had first
time around. My interpretation

meant my wild
translation. It would always
be inside and against.

You should see a girl's body outside
her dress but not be able
to say what you have seen.

That is decorum. I can't remember
whether my mother said this:
imitation

does not copy material but continues
it, giving shape
to the spirit of its making, as if the mind

at last became a pair of hands.

And if a god said this, remember: I am using my own
mouth to say what he has said.

THE PHOTOGRAPHER

Because he spends all day looking at the images he finds
beautiful, no, because he spends
all day looking for those images in the visible
world, he is not ashamed of looking for a long time
at something he finds beautiful that is not an image.
Green apple on the white desk,
he stares at it, no, he looks at it like he wants to eat.
If I were the photographer, I'd consider the color
before the shape, I'd think and try to conjure,
to keep, in my head, that shade of green.
If it were a sound it would be a *ping*,
the kind used by submarine commanders to sound
a presence at the epic depth such vessels
occupy, the shade of green that has a bit of yellow
in it, somewhere in between the yellow lily
and the yellow lily's leaf. Then I'd think about
the rotten place on the lower right-hand side,

at the base, which does not right now keep
the apple from balancing, from somehow
standing up. Green-apple green.
Now watch me put his image in my throat.

Early memories dim with their recollection: the fern
    kingdom
rebuilt when the rest of the fence-wrecking foliage got
    ripped
out, sweet William in abundance at another edge of the
    lawn-dominated
yard, dozens of kinds of once-cultivated blooms running
    wild abandoning
their original plot, like the misbehaving setter released to
    run
after some human food she could smell on the beach.
    Look how I am letting them
go for you, calling them up, like trellises the twilight
clings to, pointing out so many things left out by day,
    pointing
out the population of unspotted ladybugs perching at
    times with visible
nonchalance on the thorns that accompany the roses,

better than any terribly infernal noon or cool
loose morning light could ever do. It is the one thing
I have discovered I can give you that requires
my own diminishing but does not call
attention to my body as a source of pity, at least
for very long. And so, I give them
to you freely, as I have been told to do,
these stories that are now barely stories.
Tell me what I know when I've forgotten it.

NEW PARABLE

Was birth the worst thing, or the first
time a body left your bed? I dozed off into that
question like a person reading a text
too closely to be understood, and when I woke,
I remembered I had seen a woman working
in the field, and by her posture, simply by the way
she went at it, bent over, halfhearted, like a person
no longer wanted, no longer working
hard, I could tell, as she pulled garlic
by the root, those stalks streaked with purple, which I
    could see,
someone had abandoned her,
necessity all over the forced leisure of her hands,
still covered with that good dirt caked in company.

I will take the story of his kindness and sequester it
from all the other stories of his character: his bluntness
of speech, the time he thought me selfish.
Or the Christmas I gave him music, and he gave me a stone.
Gorgeous strains of green in the granite, eye could search
for a pattern forever and never find it, but where would I
    put it?
So it is with friendship. He kept it in his house.
I was told, *Do not store up what's precious.*

Years later, the same argument
about what to eat and drink
for hours. Those in elected
positions whirl around those positions
like petals on a flower. At night,
the story of the accident gets told again, this time,
the greatest dramatic pause follows the rescuer
walking away. I say it has been years,
years, I say, to any flower that will
listen, to our excuses for lilies, a flower
I've never actually seen.

THE REWARD

If you love those who love you, what reward do you have?
And so I went into the world, determined not to love
the black lizard doing his mighty push-up on the middle
     crossbeam
of the three-pronged trellis any more than I cared for
the dented Marine truck no longer useful, save for sitting
     in and remembering
the Marine who left it in this used-to-be-an-ocean,
     remembering his time
in a unit devoted to the design, cultivation, and placement
of smaller explosives, and the detonation of those devices,
     though the cleanup
got left to another person in another truck.

On one side of the scale, a dish the size of a fist
with a pinch of mint the same amount
as the largest tooth of your youngest child. The man
removes it, replaces it with another dish, two pinches of
    cumin
ground from the seed and roasted over a fire just hot
enough to burn a light orange for at least the time it took to
    tell
the story of your birth to a stranger who knew nothing of
    your
country, not even its name. The man removes it, sets it next
    to the mint. In a small
tin cup, he places a handful of dill, so fresh it smells like
    seaweed from the earth.
The soft plant looks cool and sea-shaped, an imagination of
    ocean
submerges it, a little sea imagined right there, in the cup.
Against each the man has weighed a piece of paper with a
    list

of all your transgressions from the time you mixed
up Mother and Father to the long way you took home
to see the sunset, just to be alone, avoiding chores
until they were too late to do. Then someone comes
who wants you to see the sunset, tells you to rejoice.
He tells you, *Keep your spices for yourself*. To flavor water,
to grill your game across the coals you only lit
to keep you warm, to fill a vase with dill and call it *flowers*.
But when the sun goes down, you wonder what it weighs.

In those days I began to see light under every
bushel basket, light nearly splitting
the sides of the bushel basket. Light came
through the rafters of the dairy where the grackles
congregated like well-taxed citizens
untransfigured even by hope. Understand I was the one
underneath the basket. I was certain I had nothing to say.
When I grew restless in the interior,
the exterior gave.

Man my mother never
voted for, I hear you lived
in the basement
apartment, underneath
mine, in Somerville,
Massachusetts.
Crocuses, then daffodils,
and the usual volunteers
of natives, even
the groundcover blooms.
Health care is a right
and marriage a gateway
to what most
people want at three
in the morning. Thank you
for believing in
global warming. I love
how you look at your wife.

Let's talk about airport
security. The last
time I went through
an agent pulled the clip
from my hair himself.
An abalone shell
from the coast of California
still shines pink
the color of labia
in Massachusetts, where
Dickinson loved
the circle so much
it became an American
landscape. The day I
realized my mother
would never vote
for you, I taught
a classroom a poem
by Robinson Jeffers: a beautiful
woman puts on
the skin of a lion, and runs
into the cypresses on a rainy
evening, after her aged
father has died

so she will get shot
by the son
of her brutal husband.
When I call my brother
he doesn't pick up his
cell and my father
goes to the ordination of
a priest, for pleasure,
on a Saturday,
with a new wife.
Man of state, how did
you study, late
into the night, or at a diner,
the whole day a list
of errands? Is the economy
a paycheck or happiness?
What I can't buy
the dead I buy my friend
whose child shook
with seizures
all fall, and the crease
in the peach tulips edged in golden-
rod yellow lets in a bit
of light, then a streak

of fade, and though the bouquet
may stay less
time she'll love
it more for
opening like that. Into
the ground, under a pine,
chosen for its thick
root potentially, in another
generation, upending
not hers but the next-
door stone, even in that purchase
we worried about ourselves and not
another, took note of and
moved straight over their loss, though
the tree might decide to hold
its ground and go deeper, not out,
she went and you
became president. Obama,
I am closer now
if I never meet you or stand
in the same room
with you than I'll ever be
again to my mother.
The air you breathe

parts molecules and circulates towards
my body, towards the state
where I pay my rent.
The waste you make enters
the stream of general waste, and she
past waste makes nothing.

I climbed a mountain and the air constricted breathing—
the terrain of the free spirit, that creature
so dedicated to surmounting that the mountain,
its hanging glacier, its granite slabs cut through
by the trail, its heaps of rocks blocking reasonable
access to the turquoise lake beneath, its wildflowers
with their fraying lackadaisical paintbrushes,
went by in my eyes so quickly I never truly left
the not-yet-turning aspens, carved by local lovers
who loved themselves so much they stayed right
there with their knives until they finished their names.

DATE

The waitress in the oceanfront
restaurant admires the choices of the couple
sitting by the gaslit fireplace:
fisherman's stew with saffron and fresh
cilantro, and, for the woman,
linguine with clams. He was not born here.

When couples come here,
it is supposed to be romantic, they ask to sit up front
by the window, often it's the woman
who asks, and if it's a new couple
and the feeling between them fresh,
she will say, *I love this place.*

This time, the man says it: he likes this place.
He means he likes the ocean, always here,
and so the fish they serve tastes fresh.
Good fishermen hang full nets in front
of trusty boats to show their haul just like a couple
holds hands in public. He asks the woman

if she likes it too, and then the woman
smiles, not because she likes the place,
its black-and-white photos and rotting couple
of oars poised above the fire pit, *taken here*,
the photos seem to say, old men standing in front
of crafts that survived gales in no fresh

air that hasn't lived with salt, no fresh
catch without a hook, no woman
in the picture, or one, looking a bit too proud, in front.
What she likes is that he likes this place.
The ocean happened here
first, though pioneers claim they did, and a couple

had coves named after themselves. "That couple
chose the fire and not the view. Asked what was fresh
and then they ordered it," you can almost hear
the waitress saying to another woman.
"As if to put love in its place,
they looked at each other, not out front."

I hear, in the garden,
fresh from making the ocean, God found a place
for a couple at the front, and the woman paid.

You have an organ shaped like a heart
that's not a heart. Poppies by the highway grow the color
of traffic cones and look like fistfuls of firecrackers
before the snap and pop. The weatherman wonders about
   the water

table the way a vintner cultivates
a public understanding of the promise of his grapes,
selling something, the story stands in for all
that hasn't been, anesthetizing years

of drought. The surgeon likes to win. What's wrong with girls
like you he says he can fix. He turns his hands
into a picture you can understand of who you are
inside, more legible than a photo, since it moves.

But he must take you under!
The day after, the neighbor's wisteria, April
edition, hangs
in doubles like lungs. That's how you see it—one day,

a lattice strewn with snuggling bright *almosts*,
those pairs in fine negotiation about their bloom.
The next, twin sacs of one working system.
But how the purple weighs down the apparatus,

making the white seem weightless when it's not,
when seriously each petal weighs the same,
and all of them together not that much,
and not too much for a good fence to take.

Or is that you, again, with your descriptions,
fresh from the hospital, fresh from the earth?
What good comes of saying how things are? The surgeon did.
Then he told you how they must be changed.

The baker at the edge of the cemetery
displays the raspberry and almond tarts
that look delicious all across the city.
His visual arrangement beckons hunger.
On a rainy day the berries glisten.

It is not like either of us to gorge
ourselves on sweets. A coin
sat in your throat. Your throat, the day before
coated in some liquor of the south.
Drink slowly, and with two cubes of ice,

and as you drink turn sunshine into blood.
Somewhere an angel worth your faith
throws his leg over a casement. Over his right shoulder
ascends a crescent moon. The coin in your throat, an
    understanding
of how much more you were entitled to.

I would take any palliative measure,
you said in the gallery as we settled
into a wordy astonishment at the dead toreador's
two white-socked feet pointing into space
just north of the outstretched drama of his cloak,

its pink as delicate as a girlish wound.
I believe you have been through enough.
The coin you spent is just a taste of what
the treacherous and fecund earth will cough
up when you stare its sweetness in the face.

Turning in the middle seat of the Country
Squire
wrapped in one blanket and clutching
another,
trying to find some way
to lie down
and look out the window at the same
time,
home sick from school.
A year later, I'd see the smoke
horizon pushing
against the ceiling
of my first airplane, my mother's lips
parted in pleasure. In the Advent
part of the liturgical
calendar, Christ isn't born
yet, and everyone in the roads
takes leave to return

to the homes of their fathers.
In the pageant I didn't
get the role I wanted, innkeeper,
because the month before
I'd been the sun.
At the center of the solar
system, no one spoke up
but me, and my mother
cut pieces of orange
and yellow poster board into rays
for a circle
the size of the table.
I don't know if I was carried
to the car. I thought,
The snake might be
at school.
In the black space I could
make by closing
my eyes and wanting,
I saw him taken
out of his cage and placed
on the taped circumference.
I knew that
would never happen.

From the back
of the seat I wailed,
Where are we going?
You go through the richest
places to get to
the poorest, she said, her
sunglasses on top
of her head, a quilted
jacket with a print of birds
with flowers
in their mouths, red and green
for the holiday against black
piped in pink trim.
Sometimes healing is a kind
of laundry, a reminder
that the earlier state
was better but not good.
The radio played
"Yesterday." At a stop
sign I heard
my mother crying.
John Lennon has been
shot, she said, John
Lennon is dead.

Who was he? I asked.
He made a record
called *Double Fantasy*
but that's not why
I'm crying, I'm crying
because of the Beatles.
"Yesterday" was done.
Next came "Working
Class Hero." We looked
at the stop sign
for a very long time
and drove on. Music,
it was not sadness
that gave birth to you,
but astonishment.
The person whose body
I lived inside loved
something before me
and drove around singing.

The eye is the lamp of the body, so I tried
to make a world where all I ate was light. A butterfly
completes a similar labor in the summer
garden, beating its wings slowly like a healthy
person, the kind who runs for fun, could
run from an attacker, eats greens in the same
quantity as the salty meats the storytelling part
of us appears to favor. I couldn't decide
whether I wanted to stay alive or go
faster, they appeared to contradict each other, I tried
in all I did to eat light. I left the argument
about the difference between a slave and a servant
on the table, though I think what I think is that
consent to servitude is as much a fiction as a butterfly
having a nervous breakdown because of the beauty
of the lavender. The longer your hunger takes
to find a shape, the longer you can hold it. Consider the
    butterfly,

only at rest in the middle of consumption, but even
then preparing for departure, for disappearance,
closing in the middle of the landscape.
Trying to manage a world in which all you eat
is light is difficult. Labor, and the lungs should be like wings
of a butterfly beating, closing slowly, the moonlight
tensing the edge of each, almost lifting the edge of each
towards the middle distance. So all that I consume
can make me healthy, illuminate my throat
and the interstate of my digestive tract
with what a butterfly's been swimming in.

HONEYMOON SUITE

When the light retreats,

            the landscape focuses

but with no depth,

            the ferryboat moving

into the dark—

            you're trying to find

a version of slowness

for the soul

accustomed to hurry

ravens

chasing each other, and the fourteenth-

floor window cuts through a midsection

of glacier

You said

Happy Holidays to the woman

in the market and she wanted *Merry*

Christmas

That's what you wanted too—

a spark

in the nick of hay

the kings on their knees

and people confused

about a beautiful child

A weight on the world

cars moving but muffled

the roads indistinguishable

at last, from the rest of Earth

Now the harbor our television

eating dinner on our knees
waiting for the ship to Gustavus

to sail into broken ice

All good people are like ferryboats

They work

with current

until they can't then go

against it bravely

diligent not faithful

capsized by excess

        untroubled

by weight

        The bore tide south

of the city brings Pacific

                into the estuary

        the urge to move closer

        the ocean moving at cross-purposes

with the river's current, the river that makes

a funneled bay, an *arm*

goes the idiom, and you love

        the idiom, the starfish

of the idiom, the amputation

of the body

for water a body

would never survive

        you heard

about the newlywed

who didn't, who went towards

the tide, who stranded

herself in muddy shallows, you heard

        the legend and sorrow of that story, imagined

the groom and his actual personality

and where

then do you put the desire

for property, the entitlement

to china

with a pattern of rosebuds and daisies bound

with grosgrain —

One train clears

the tracks for the real train that moves

goods from earth to moving water   you heard

in the vibration

of the metal   something about a reign

coming where debt could be abolished,

everyone save the lover

and the beloved in right

relation, and those two

skewered forever on top

of each other only

because they wanted to

                              Where

do your people come from?

On Kodiak Island, mine

are waiting, if you mean

those who share my name

the mountain rising into its own

cloud of falling snow

but if you bring

a wordlessness with you, any sound

can lift that mountain out

Each exceptional

person like a ferryboat

everyone waits for them

moving around in their lighted cabins

you can see

an exceptional person until they are entirely

gone

Ravens

turn into seabirds

when they cross the border

of the harbor, then turn

back

        whether or not the pink

outlasts the morning,

        as if the purpose had ever been warmth,

the future turns

        to a perimeter

like a honeymoon suite.

He wanted them to give him money. He asked
for a massive tape machine
to collect the music of Morocco.
The book got made into a movie.
When I watched it, I saw a breast,
the first in my life that didn't
belong to my family. In the Central
Valley, my husband teaches
his students. *Husband*,
a word from the Normans.
Younger than the word *wife*.
This morning we had to borrow money.
It made me want to say
to him, "Did you know
the things you'd have to do
if you came to my country?"
What kind of traveler are you?
Oppositional. I want what I didn't have

before. Today I want my husband
to come home in the middle
of the day and sit here
at the kitchen table
and act like nothing bad could be
for very long. Tea in the Sahara,
a china cup with a spray
of pink rosebud importing
a strange and unacknowledged humidity
into the windswept scene.
Sand sediments in the saucer.
They wanted to do that in the novel.
In times like these, no one asks for sugar.

NOTE

ACKNOWLEDGMENTS

NOTE

"ECHO BEFORE THE ECHO"

Up to this time Echo still had a body,
She was not merely voice.

(Ovid, *Metamorphoses*, Book III,
lines 362–363, trans. Rolfe Humphries)

ACKNOWLEDGMENTS

Grateful acknowledgment is given to the editors of the following publications, in which some of these poems previously appeared or will appear, sometimes in slightly different form: *The American Poetry Review, Cherry Tree, Iron Horse Literary Review, Octopus, Poetry, Poetry Northwest, T: The New York Times Style Magazine, Tuesday: An Art Project, Third Coast,* and *West Branch.*

"New Parable" is included in *The Echoing Green: Poems of Fields, Meadows, and Grasses,* Knopf/Everyman's Library Pocket Poets.

"Pleasure" appeared on the Academy of American Poets' Poem-a-Day on October 25, 2013.

I thank the American Academy of Arts and Letters, the Foundation for Contemporary Arts, and the Radcliffe Institute for Advanced Study for generous support during the years in which these poems were written. I thank those who have read this book closely and helped me find it—you know who you are, dear companions. And I thank my friends in Massachusetts, for giving me a home in that state that is not my home.